The *Guide to Success* series was developed to help those who do not have the money, time, or inclination to invest in post-secondary courses, but who have the desire to grow and to better themselves. We know that most people lead busy lives. Accordingly, we have designed the guides to be succinct. The guides are a great source of information and invaluable reference tools. Use them to assist you on your road to success.

To order more *Guides to Success* visit us at *www.bisconsulting.ca*

Titles currently available in the
Guide to Success Series:

Success

Leadership

Management

Watch for exciting new additions
to the *Guide to Success* Series

SUCCESS

Principles
and Strategies
for Success

Second Printing

Published in Canada by
   Business Improvement Solutions Inc.
   180, 150 Chippewa Road, Sherwood Park, Alberta T8A 6A2
   Telephone (780) 410-1660   Fax (780) 410-1659   www.bisconsulting.ca

Library and Archives Canada Cataloguing in Publication

MacDonald, Dan (Daniel Roderick)
       Success: principles and strategies / written by Daniel R. MacDonald and Carmen L. DeLisle; edited by Karen Hoffmann-Zak. — 1st ed.

(Guide to success)
Includes bibliographical references.
ISBN 978-1-897346-04-4

   1. Success. 2. Self-actualization (Psychology) 3. Success in business. I. DeLisle, Carmen II. Hoffmann-Zak, Karen III. Title. IV. Series.

   BF637.S8M347 2007   158.1   C2007-900242-0

Edited by Karen Hoffmann-Zak, Toronto
Book design and layout by Ingénieuse Productions, Edmonton

Printed in Canada

Use this book as a reference to help you achieve success.
By using the principles within this book, you increase your
likelihood of realizing your dreams. It's all up to you, however,
and so results cannot be guaranteed. Your ability to succeed
depends on many factors including, but not limited to,
the feasibility of your goals, your perseverance, and
your effort. It's a truism that getting there is half
the fun. May your journey and destination
be fascinating and fulfilling.

Introduction

*He has achieved success who
has lived well, laughed often and
loved much; who has gained the respect
of intelligent men, the trust of pure women
and the love of little children; who has filled
his niche and accomplished his task;
who has left the world better than he
found it, whether by an improved poppy,
a perfect poem, or a rescued soul;
who has never lacked appreciation
of Earth's beauty or failed to
express it; who has looked
for the best in others and given
them the best he had; whose life was
inspiration; his memory a benediction.*

~ Bessie Anderson Stanley, poet
often attributed to Ralph Emerson Waldo

TAKE A MOMENT TO IMAGINE YOUR FUTURE. IT'S FIVE years from now and you are in better physical shape than you have ever been in your life. Many great friends surround you. You have a happy, healthy, and loving family. You have no financial stress in your life. You have plenty of time to enjoy the things that you like to do. Energetic and enthusiastic, you cannot wait to start each day. Sound too good to be true? Is this reality possible for you? You decide.

There are no secrets to success. Great success is possible for anyone, anywhere, to achieve. It is possible for you, but it all depends on you. You are the reason for all of your victories, as well as your woes. The choices you make determine what is possible in your life. Your past actions and choices resulted in your current career, income, net worth, and relationships. You made all of the decisions. Your life is the sum of all of your choices to date. Even inaction is a choice that will affect your life.

If you are ready to choose success and are truly willing to do what is necessary to achieve it, open your mind to the ideas within this book, and to the potential within you.

"To dream anything that you want to dream, that is the beauty of the human mind. To do anything that you want to do, that is the strength of the human will. To trust yourself to test your limits, that is the courage to succeed."

~ Bernard Edmonds

Sections

"Success is

focusing the full power of

all you are on what you have

a burning desire to achieve."

~ Wilfred Peterson, author

To PRESENT KEY PRINCIPLES AND STRATEGIES OF SUCCESS, this book is divided into the following two sections:

Section 1: The Success Factors – In this section, we present and explain twelve key factors for success:

- ✔ choices
- ✔ focus
- ✔ positive attitude
- ✔ failure
- ✔ two degrees of separation
- ✔ positive habits
- ✔ act "as if"
- ✔ zero-based thinking
- ✔ self-awareness
- ✔ the power of the mind
- ✔ return on investment
- ✔ the will to succeed

By understanding and acknowledging the importance of these factors, you can increase your likelihood of achieving great success.

Section 2: Five Steps to Success – Your actions determine your level of success. These five steps can be used to help you achieve the future you have always dreamed about.

- ✔ define success
- ✔ ask why
- ✔ assess your situation
- ✔ determine a course of action
- ✔ chart your progress

The
Success
Factors

"Success is no exclusive club.

It is open to each individual who

has the courage to choose his own goal

and go after it."

~ Howard Whitman

THERE IS NO QUICK AND EASY WAY TO BECOME successful. It requires work and perseverance. The good news is that if you persevere and work long and hard on the things that matter, you can succeed. To ease your journey, we identify twelve factors that, once learned and applied, will greatly increase your ability to achieve lasting success.

Success Factor 1: Choices

*"The greatest power that a person possesses
is the power to choose."* [1]
~ *J. Martin Kohe, author and psychologist*

Every day you make thousands of choices that determine your life's path: each person whom you do or do not greet, each smile you give or withhold, each person with whom you do or do not make eye contact, each word of encouragement or discouragement you utter, each time you speak or stay silent when something needs to be said. Think through your day. Did you make the best choice in every situation?

Whether or not you like the results of your choices, you are 100 percent responsible for the actions you choose. Realizing that is the first step to success. By choosing as you do, you are also fully responsible for your happiness. Truly understanding and internalizing this truth is like a "get out of jail free" pass from your mental cell.

Think about the last time someone angered you at work. Think about all the ill feelings that resulted. Think of all the frustrated and angry looks and words exchanged. Now, realize that you chose those feelings. You decided to be angry. You decided to let the situation get the best of you. No one can make you feel a certain way. No one can choose your feelings. The ability to control other people's emotions does not exist. Yet, every day, thousands of people say things like, "He really makes me mad"; "She hurt my feelings"; or "He embarrassed me." All of these statements are false. More accurate statements would be, "I chose to let him get to me"; "I chose to feel bad because of what she said"; and "I allowed myself to be embarrassed by his actions." You choose! You decide your feelings! You determine your response by how you interpret a situation and by how you decide to react to it. You are responsible for your life.

It is important to understand that your choices determine how much success and happiness you achieve. How you choose to react to situations will dramatically affect your life's direction. Know that 90 percent of all people can read this book, agree with it, and then make no attempt to accomplish what they really want or hope for in life. If you are among the other 10 percent of people, then you are one of the few that can choose to build a better life. The choice and responsibility are yours.

Success Factor 2: Focus

"Our thoughts create our reality—where we put our focus is the direction we tend to go."
~ Peter McWilliams, author (1950-2000)

The ability to focus your efforts is fundamental to success. When you focus on something, you bring more of it into your life. Therefore, it is important to choose your focus wisely.

Focus on the Important

When you focus on end results and accomplishing tasks critical to success, you are productive in an exponential way rather than a marginal way. Unfortunately, many people act efficiently with poor results. They accomplish many tasks, but most of these tasks don't affect their goals. As a result, they dramatically reduce their ability to realize success.

One way to overcome the tendency to focus on unimportant tasks is to question whether or not an action brings you closer to achieving your goals. Socrates' words, though centuries old, seem to reinforce this advice. When asked, "How do you get to Mount Olympus?" he replied, "Just make sure every step you take is in that direction."

Continually asking yourself whether or not you are moving towards fulfilling your goals can be a powerful way to stop wasting precious time on unnecessary or unproductive tasks.

Consider the habit of watching television. The average person watches three hours of TV a day. One hour of this viewing time often comes from 'surfing and settling.' Unable to find a program we like, we settle on one of the remaining options. If, instead, we chose to watch one less hour of TV a day, we would gain 365 hours a year, the equivalent of 10 additional workweeks. Imagine what could be achieved if we annually spent the equivalent of 10 full-time workweeks improving our future. This time could be used to accomplish important and meaningful tasks that would dramatically improve our quality of life.

To positively influence your level of success, it is important to acquire the following new habit—before or while doing something, ask yourself, "Will this activity help me to succeed in my goals?" Take the time to answer this question. Once the habit of asking and answering this question is established and practiced consistently, it becomes easier to avoid unproductive, meaningless tasks. This allows you to focus your thoughts on getting what you really want out of life.

Focus on the Positive

Napoleon Hill, author and a leader of the personal success movement, understood the importance of focusing on the positive. Hired by Andrew Carnegie to write a simple formula for success that average people could use, Hill interviewed some of the most successful people of his time: Thomas Edison, Alexander Graham Bell, Henry Ford, George Eastman, Theodore Roosevelt, John D. Rockefeller, Charles Schwab, Woodrow Wilson, and William H. Taft, to name a few. He captured their words and wisdom in multiple books on achieving success.

Auto-suggestion was one of the key principles Hill wrote about. "Auto-suggestion is self-suggestion," he stated. "It is the agency of communication between that part of the mind where conscious thought takes place, and that which serves as the seat of action for the subconscious mind."[2] He continued, "Through the dominating thoughts which one permits to remain in the conscious mind (whether these thoughts be negative or positive is immaterial), the principle of auto-suggestion voluntarily reaches the subconscious mind and influences it with these thoughts."[3] The subconscious mind, he said, works day and night to make these thoughts a reality. If we focus on our fears, our subconscious mind acts to make them real. If we focus on our desires and wishes, our subconscious mind will work to make these real. It is our choice to make our focus—and, therefore, our reality—either positive or negative.

When we focus on having a good day at work, what happens? We have a good day. If we think that we will be tired once we finish another long day at the office, how do we feel at the end of the day? Exhausted? Have you ever noticed that the people who say things like, "I always get into bad relationships"; "I never have any luck keeping a job"; or "I always get sick when the weather changes"; are usually right? They consistently focus on all of the things that could go wrong and subconsciously make these thoughts their reality.

The good news is that people can choose to focus on positive outcomes, making these come true instead. People who say things like, "I always get great promotions"; "I never have any trouble making friends"; or "I always find great deals"; make this their reality. Remember that you choose the thoughts you focus upon. You can either choose to focus on positive or negative thoughts. Whatever your choice, your focus will affect your future.

Focus on the Results

When aspiring to succeed, you have two choices: you can think about the effort required to achieve your goals, or you can think about the results of achieving them. This choice is critical. Many people stop themselves long before making an action plan for achieving success. That's because they focus on the work involved instead of on the positive final result.

Consider the example of a man trying to lose weight. He has a very important decision to make that will greatly influence whether or not he succeeds: he can focus on the effort required to lose weight, or he can focus on the outcome of losing weight. He can focus on his new, lean, toned physique; the positive attention he may receive as a result of it; and the increased energy he will feel. Or, he can focus on all of the cardiovascular training, weight lifting, dieting, and early mornings that stand between him and a new, healthier build. By focusing on the work instead of on the end results, he will likely exhaust himself before even getting off the couch!

When you focus on the positive outcome instead of on the effort required to achieve this outcome, you significantly increase your ability to achieve success.

Success Factor 3: Positive Attitude

"Things turn out best for the people who
make the best out of the way things turn out."
~ Art Linkletter, radio broadcaster and television personality

Attitude is the general feeling we have and display towards someone or something. Attitudes can be positive or negative. The attitudes we choose greatly influence whether and how well we shall succeed.

A person with a positive attitude can choose positive, rather than negative, feelings, emotions, thoughts, and reactions. This person chooses to see silver linings, while a person with a negative attitude sees only clouds.

Attitude is more important than many people realize. A positive attitude can help you get a promotion even when you're competing against colleagues more experienced and educated than you. People are often eager to help and support those with great attitudes. A positive attitude can make all the difference between constantly feeling tired, stressed, and miserable, or energetic, happy, and full of life. Attitude is everything.

Success Factor 4: Failure

"Failure is the tuition you pay for success."
~ *Walter Brunell*

Successful people know that failure precedes success. They know that failure is a necessary part of the learning experience and, accordingly, see it as an opportunity for improvement—not as an end. They know that if they never fail, it means they have never really tried anything. To them, this is much more detrimental than failing.

Great success and failure go hand in hand. Babe Ruth, famed baseball player, did not only hit home runs; he also struck out. During his amazing career, topping the American League home run leader board 12 out of 14 years, he also earned six spots on the League's yearly strikeout leader list. Basketball star Michael Jordan once said, "I've missed more than 9,000 shots in my career. I've lost almost 300 games. Twenty-six times, I've been trusted to take the game winning shot and missed. I've failed over and over and over again in my life. And that is why I succeed."

Many of today's most celebrated inventions come from product failures and customer problems. For instance, the Alto computer, invented by researchers at the Xerox Palo Alto Research Center, never became a commercially viable product. It did, however, introduce the world to the graphic user interface, an invention that helped spawn the wildly successful Windows operating system. Thomas Edison failed more than one thousand times while attempting to invent the light bulb. Instead of viewing his unsuccessful attempts as failures, he said, "We now know a thousand ways not to make a light bulb."

It is important to view failure as a stepping stone to success. When we do this, we learn from our mistakes, and continue moving closer to our goals.

Success Factor 5: Two Degrees of Separation

> *"Sometimes it's the smallest decisions*
> *that can change our lives forever."*
> ~ *Keri Russell, actress, in her role as TV's Felicity*

Two degrees of separation is a principle that states that a small change habitually practiced can dramatically change one's future. By changing your course in life slightly, say by a mere two degrees, you can change your future exponentially. Consider a ship leaving Sydney, Australia for Vancouver, Canada. If the ship changes course by just two degrees every 2000 kilometres, it will be approximately 850 nautical miles or 1576 kilometres off course. It will arrive near Santa Barbara, California instead of Vancouver. This would be an unexpected detour.

Consider the task of building wealth. With the help of compound interest, we can dramatically increase our wealth over time. In 40 years, a two-dollar-a-day investment, earning an annual rate of return of 10 percent, would produce a nest egg of just over $390,000. If you invest $4 each day, in 40 years, you would have over $782,000. And how much money would you have in 40 years from a $6 per day investment? More than a million dollars! This example clearly illustrates how much your future level of success can vary depending on the small habitual changes you make today.

Success Factor 6: Positive Habits

"The common denominator of success—the secret of success of every man who has ever been successful—lies in the fact that he formed the habit of doing things that failures don't like to do."
~ *Albert Gray, former official of the Prudential Insurance Company of America*

Habits are behaviours so automatic that we tend not to think about them. Habits are like automatic pilot controls in an airplane. The habits you choose can powerfully affect your life, as they can dramatically affect your level of success. If you choose positive habits, you can change your life for the better. If you choose negative habits, your habits may control the direction of your life, and the results could be devastating.

To illustrate the power of habit, cross your arms in front of your body. Look at your arms: from habit, the dominant arm usually ends up on top. Now, consciously try to cross your arms again, this time with the opposite arm on top. Does this feel uncomfortable? Some people have a difficult time even doing it. This is what it feels like when you start a new habit: awkward. But over time, the new habit will feel as natural as placing your dominant arm on top.

When you want to eliminate a bad habit, consciously replace it with a new and better habit. Be aware, however, that when changing your habits, things usually get worse before they get much better. This results from your transition through the four stages of competency when learning a new behaviour: unconscious incompetence, conscious incompetence, conscious competence, and unconscious competence. During the first stage—unconscious incompetence—people do not know how to perform the behaviour and do not realize that they need to learn such behaviour. During the second stage—conscious incompetence—people realize their deficiency but do not know how to perform the desired behaviour. During the third stage—conscious competence—people have successfully adapted the desirable behaviour. During the fourth and final stage—unconscious competence—people have successfully made the behaviour a habit and no longer need to focus on it to perform.[4]

As we learn new habits, we move through the four stages of competency. Our performance of the desired behaviour follows the shape of the letter 'J.' Economists refer to this as the "J" curve principle: after a change, our progress follows the shape of the letter "J"—first downwards, then dramatically upwards.[5]

If you have the tenacity to develop and maintain good habits, you will enjoy future success! It's in your best interest to replace these bad habits with good ones.

Adopt a New Positive Habit

Dramatically change your chances of success by adopting great habits. Consider your current life and what it will look like many years from now if you develop the following new habits today:

- ✔ invest $10 each and every day;
- ✔ read a non-fiction book every month about personal development or your field of expertise;
- ✔ spend 30 uninterrupted minutes daily with the people you love;
- ✔ improve your diet;

✔ exercise for 30 minutes daily; and

✔ perform an altruistic deed every day.

Think how profoundly these actions would change your life over the course of 20, 30 or 40 years. You can cultivate literally hundreds of good habits that can dramatically improve your life. The key is finding and developing the habits that will improve your chances of future success. Remember: tenacious and disciplined people succeed. Start building valuable habits today!

Success Factor 7: Act "As If"

> *"Act as if you have already achieved*
> *your goal and it is yours."*
> ~ *Dr. Robert Anthony, self-help author*

For excellent advice on achieving success, reflect on William Shakespeare's words, and "assume a virtue if you have it not."[6] William James, an American psychologist and philosopher, concurred with the wisdom of this advice, noting that "by regulating the action, which is under the more direct control of the will, we can indirectly regulate the feeling, which is not."[7] James realized that if we act a certain way, we alter how we feel. Consequently, if we choose to act happy, in time we will be happy. Caution: the reverse is true, too.

When applying the "as if" principle to success, it is important to act truly successful, not just to assume an air of success. If you simply go out and buy Armani suits and a BMW, you will not be successful. In fact, you will probably experience less success as you struggle to pay for these status symbols. To effectively use the "as if" principle to achieve success, your actions must mimic commonly demonstrated characteristics of truly successful people: passion, perseverance, diligence, dedication, and focus.

Success Factor 8: Zero-based Thinking

"The significant problems we have cannot be solved at the same level of thinking with which we created them"
~ Albert Einstein, renowned physicist and genius (1879-1955)

Sometimes, on the road to success, it becomes difficult to make decisions. To work through these situations, Brian Tracy, author of more than 30 bestsellers on career and personal development, recommends using a technique called zero-based thinking.[8] Zero-based thinking is the result of clearing one's mind of all distractions and influences, so that one can focus on making an optimal decision.

Zero-based thinking can be applied to many aspects of your life. You only need to ask yourself what Brian Tracy calls the zero-based thinking question: "Knowing what I now know, if I was not now doing this, would I start it up again today?"[9] In terms of your career, you can ask yourself, "If I didn't have my current job, would I start it today, knowing what I now know?" If your answer is "no," then you clearly know what to do. With this knowledge, you can immediately take steps towards finding a more fulfilling career.

By using zero-based thinking, you can set aside all the distractions that normally prevent you from making the best possible decisions quickly. This strategy will help you to clear the distractions from your path to happiness and success.

Success Factor 9: Self-awareness

"The fish only knows that it lives in the water, after it is already on the river bank. Without our awareness of another world out there, it would never occur to us to change."

~ Unknown

Self-awareness is being fully conscious of our feelings, attitudes, and actions, and their effects. The higher our level of self-awareness, the better our understanding of concepts, situations, and our own personal reality. Self-awareness allows us to further know and understand our habits and actions, greatly improving our ability to determine which of our actions benefit us and which do not.

To be successful, we must be aware of our tendency to make excuses for not achieving our goals. Once we stop making excuses for not doing things that bring us closer to our goals, we can accelerate our journey to success. Tragically, many of us continually make excuses for why we cannot realize our dreams. We exhaust a lot of mental energy inventing excuses to justify our mediocrity. Ironically, the smarter we are, the better we are at making excuses. As awareness increases, we stop looking for reasons why things cannot be done and start finding ways they can be done.

Have you ever listened to people say, "I wish I had lots of money," or "It would be nice to have millions"? While many people who say these things are trying to rise above poverty and unthinkable circumstances, there are others who, while wishing for millions, spend all their disposable income on vacations, new campers, boats, cars, bigger homes, or other material possessions. At the same time, they often complain that they never save any money because they can't afford to do so. Such people often do not comprehend the effects of their actions. They do not realize that by continuing to spend all their money, they will never achieve financial freedom, let alone their big dreams.

Gaining Self-Awareness

Obviously, we should seek a high level of self-awareness. Two ways to accomplish this are to answer revealing questions about ourselves and to ask others what they think of us.

Ask Revealing Questions of Ourselves

To gain greater self-awareness, ask yourself the following questions:

1. What are my fears and how do they affect my life?
2. Do I choose the best emotional reaction to every situation?
3. Do I surround myself with people that I want to emulate?
4. Am I truly happy with my life?

Answering questions like these goes a long way towards improving self-awareness.

Others' Perceptions of Us

We gain higher levels of self-awareness by seeing ourselves through the eyes of others. To understand other people's perceptions of us, we need to question them. We may be surprised by what we hear if we have the courage to ask.

Ask ten people who are close to you the following four questions. Ask them for honest answers and they will likely provide them if you are open-minded and non-defensive.

1. What are my three best qualities?
2. What are my three worst qualities?
3. What are my top three strengths?
4. What are my top three weaknesses?

The answers to these questions may reveal what you need to focus your efforts upon in order to achieve greater success.

Success Factor 10: The Power of the Mind

"Our deepest fear is not that we are inadequate. Our deepest fear is that we are powerful beyond measure. It is our light, not our darkness that most frightens us. We ask ourselves, Who am I to be brilliant, gorgeous, talented, fabulous? Actually, who are you not to be?"[10]

~ *Marianne Williamson*, author
(often attributed to Nelson Mandela)

The mind's incredible power is hard to comprehend. It is difficult to believe that our minds are so powerful—and, consequently, so are we. Every day our brains perform literally thousands of functions including

- ✔ regulating our body temperature, breathing rate, heart rate, digestion, and level of alertness, attention, and arousal;

- ✔ analyzing sensory data to make sense of our world;

- ✔ allowing us to move, manipulate objects, and react to stimuli;

- ✔ controlling our ability to learn, interpret, and recall information, form thoughts, make decisions, reason, think logically, and abstractly;

✔ enabling us to concentrate, elaborate, make judgments, and solve problems; and

✔ coordinating all of the systems of the body for proper functioning.

Our brains control everything we do. Therefore, this is only a partial list of the thousands of functions our brains command. In fact, it is impossible to comprehend the untapped depth of our brain's potential.

What does this mean to you? It means that you have unrealized potential that you can tap into to get what you want from life. If you define success as being wealthy, then you need to realize that the power to become a millionaire lies within you. Remember that your mind gives you the ability to accomplish almost anything, so focus on your dreams and your mind can help to make them come true. With the right mindset and focus, nothing can defeat you.

The Power of the Mind: An Inspirational Story

The power of the human mind is unquestionable. Look at the example of a poor, black girl born in 1954 to unwed parents in Mississippi; by her account, the most racist state in the United States at that time. What chance did this girl have? Her life did not start out easy. As a young child, she was raised by her grandmother. At age six, she went to live with her mother, and her life changed for the worse.

She was regularly beaten, raped by a cousin at age nine, and sexually abused by her uncle and a friend of the family over a five-year period. At 14, she suffered the death of her premature baby.

That year, her mother decided to put her into a home for juvenile delinquents. Luckily, the home had no room for her. Instead, she went to live with her father in Tennessee. This is when she turned her life around.

Today, this woman's net worth is reported to be $1.1 billion dollars. She has a media empire, which includes a television studio, a film production company, a magazine, and a cable network. She owns numerous properties including a $50 million mansion in California and 105 acres of beachfront property in Hawaii. Among her illustrious friends are celebrities such as Brad Pitt, Tom Hanks, John Travolta, and Stevie Wonder. This woman is Oprah Winfrey.

Oprah attributes her success to her inner power: "To come from no voice, no power—economically or otherwise—and to be able to achieve what I've been able to achieve means that only my own personal vision holds me back; that anything's possible."[11] She has also stated, "Although there may be tragedy in your life, there's always a possibility to triumph. It doesn't matter who you are, where you come from. The ability to triumph begins with you. Always, always."[12]

This is the power of the mind.

Why Many People Never Realize More of Their Mind's Power

Despite the unlimited capability of the mind, which underpins everything we do, nobody has ever realized his or her full human potential. In fact, most of us realize only a very small part of our capabilities and do not see ourselves as possessing unlimited power. Unfortunately, many people find it easier to believe limiting thoughts about themselves and their abilities. As a result, many people use their minds to find evidence to prove negative self-concepts true. This is when the common phrases, "I can't"; "It's impossible"; "There's no way"; "Maybe for you but not for me"; can be heard. People who speak this way use their mind's power to limit their own potential. Consequently, they give up on their dreams and resign themselves to mediocre lives. They have allowed themselves to reason their way out of success. They decide, "That's life," and, in so doing, make it so.

Success Factor 11: Return on Investment

"Every action we take requires an investment of time.
By carefully choosing our actions, we can achieve
the greatest possible return on our investment."

~ *Anonymous*

Time is the most important asset that we have to achieve success: we need to spend it wisely. Once time is spent—

wisely or foolishly—it is gone! As Denis Waitley, motivational speaker and consultant, wrote in his book *The Psychology of Winning,* "I would like to run a classified ad in every newspaper in the world under Lost and Found: "Lost—one twenty-four hour, twenty-four carat, golden day—each hour studded with sixty diamond minutes—each minute studded with sixty ruby seconds. But don't bother to look for it, it's gone forever—that wonderful, golden day, I lost today.""" [13]

Successful people realize this truth so they make the most of their time. For instance, consider a chore such as spring-cleaning. You can either do this yourself, or you can pay someone else to do it for you, while you invest your time elsewhere—working on your goal of financial freedom. Instead of spending six hours spring cleaning your home, you pay someone $25 an hour to do it for you. You now spend those six hours researching various stocks and mutual funds. Let's assume that you have $40,000 in your investment account. During your research, you find a few good mutual funds and stocks that have outperformed your current investments by 1.5 percent annually. By investing in these funds instead of in your current holdings, you would earn more than an additional $600 annually. After ten years, by spending only the initial $150 paid to your spring cleaner and without investing any more time, you would have accumulated more than $6,400!

As you can see, how you choose to spend your time can dramatically influence the amount you earn. Increase your level of success by seeking the best return on invested time.

Success Factor 12: The Will to Succeed

"If you have the will to win, you have achieved half your success; if you don't, you have achieved half your failure."
~ *David Ambrose*

One of the most crucial factors for success is the will to succeed. If you lack the desire and perseverance to succeed, your goals become mere words. To realize your dreams, you must be willing and able to persist against any obstacles, including naysayers who call your dreams impossible. You must be able to pick yourself up after the failures you will inevitably experience, brush yourself off, and continue. The will to succeed distinguishes achievers from dreamers.

The Will to Succeed: The James Dyson Story

In 1974, James Dyson, an engineer and inventor, took a chance. Believing in himself, he left his job to start his own business. Dyson loved to create things. After opening his own business, he first invented the Ballbarrow, a wheelbarrow that used a pneumatic ball instead of a wheel to travel effortlessly over grass and dirt. Though the Ballbarrow cost more than conventional wheelbarrows, it sold very well. Unfortunately, however, a large market did not exist for wheelbarrows.

In 1978, Dyson started another invention. He noticed that the air filter in the Ballbarrow finishing room continually became clogged. Did he call in a technician as so many of us would have done? No. He set about creating a cyclone tower to rectify the situation. This tower easily resolved the problem by exerting centrifugal forces 100,000 times stronger than the force of gravity, in order to eliminate unwanted airborne particles. Could the same technology be harnessed to improve the performance of the vacuum cleaner, he wondered. After 5 years and 5,127 prototypes, Dyson finally answered his own question. By 1984, he had successfully parlayed his answer into the creation of the world's first bagless vacuum cleaner. Unfortunately, no one wanted to buy it. He spent two long years seeking a buyer for his product in the UK. Most people would not have made it this far.

He finally found a buyer in Japan. In 1986, seven years after starting his invention, the first units sold. He licensed the technology to a Japanese company and used the proceeds to open a research centre and factory. Then, he created his patented Dual Cyclone vacuum—no small feat. During the development stage of the Dual Cyclone, with no income and enormous patent renewal fees continually needing to be paid, Dyson almost went bankrupt. As if this were not enough, his competitors copied his invention. Dyson had to persevere through a patent infringement court case lasting 18 months, just to protect the invention he worked so hard to create.[14]

Now, 31 years later, his company's products sell in 39 countries with total annual sales of £470 million.[15] Dyson has amassed a personal net worth of more than $1 billion US.[16] The long journey he endured to get his product from concept to the retail floor paid itself back handsomely and speaks volumes about his incredible perseverance and will to succeed.

Steps to Success

Success doesn't come to you… you go to it.

~ Marva Collins,
teacher, trainer, and founder of the
Westside Preparatory School

NOW THAT YOU UNDERSTAND THE FACTORS THAT are important to achieving success, it is important to act. The following section presents five steps that you can follow on your journey to success.

Step 1: Define Success

The first step to realizing success is to identify what success means to you. Usually it's a combination of health, wealth, happiness, and great people with whom to share your life. A good way to clearly determine what success means to you is to ask yourself, "If I could do anything, what would I do?" or "If I could make any dream come true, what would I dream?" Spend 30 minutes listing all of your answers to these questions. List the top 20 things that you would want if you could have or do anything.

Many people find that they start their list with items such as a big house, a summer home, a sports car, or other similar material possessions. Often, they then cite more meaningful goals.

Once you have completed your list, prioritize each item in order, from most to least important, according to how happy each accomplishment will make you. This priority list will help you to focus your efforts on achieving those things that will significantly improve your life.

Step 2: Ask Yourself Why?

Once you have determined what success means to you, ask yourself, "Why do I want to be successful?" Do you feel that you can achieve more than you currently achieve? Do you have a burning desire to be more successful? If you answered "yes" to any of these questions, then you have the impetus for success.

To increase your ability to achieve success, list all of your reasons for succeeding. Reasons might include better health, less stress, better relationships, more freedom, and more opportunities to do what you like to do most. By determining reasons for succeeding, you help build the desire, drive, and determination to persevere. Make the time to review these reasons daily. Doing so will greatly increase your ability to succeed.

Step 3: Assess Your Situation

To determine what you must do to succeed, it is important to assess your current situation. Only when you know where you are can you effectively determine the best way to get to where you want to go.

To assess your current situation, take the list that you wrote in Step 1, and write down those things that you ranked at the top of your priority list. Assess how close you currently are to accomplishing each of these objectives. You may find that you are close to achieving some, while others seem very far away. Don't be discouraged. With hard work and perseverance almost all of your goals can be achieved.

Step 4: Determine a Course of Action and Begin

Once you know where you are and where you want to be, you can determine the best route to get there. As you plan your course of action, follow these two steps:

1. Review and implement the 10 success factors. By applying these factors, you improve your results and reach your desired destination more quickly.

2. Remember that you do not have to do it on your own. Seek opinions and information from people who have successfully done what you hope to do. Read books on the subject. This may start you thinking in new and creative ways. Talk to your friends—they may offer valuable insights. Just talking your ideas through with them may help you to clarify your thoughts and inspire you to think of new ways to achieve your goals.

Once you have gathered information and shared your ideas, you should be able to determine what course of action to take. Once your plan is ready, use it immediately to take you where you want to go.

Step 5: Chart Your Progress

On your journey to success, make sure that you regularly stop to chart your progress. Are you still heading in the right direction? Did you take a wrong turn somewhere? Are you exactly where you planned to be? Answers to these questions provide you with valuable feedback.

When you reflect on where you are, you accomplish two very important tasks: you ensure that you are on the right path and you motivate yourself to continue. If you find that you have been working away and have not yet realized your goals, adjust your plans. You can consult with your sources to determine a course that will help you get back on track.

Charting your progress is also a great way to motivate yourself to continue exerting the effort needed to succeed. When you first started your journey towards success, you wrote a description of your situation and your goals. Periodically, review this description. Compare it to where you are now and to where you want to go. By seeing how far you have progressed, and how your hard work has paid off, you renew your energy and can continue moving forward.

*"Success is to be measured
not so much by the position
that one has reached in life
as by the obstacles which
he has overcome."*

*~ Booker T. Washington,
African American political leader,
educator, and author
(1856-1915)*

Conclusion

"Success is

not so much what

we have as it is

what we are." [17]

~ Jim Rohn,
motivational speaker,
business coach, and author

SUCCESS, LIKE MANY OTHER THINGS IN LIFE, IS A CHOICE. We challenge you to choose not to let life pass you by. Life is not a spectator sport—don't just sit on the sidelines watching other people live fully each day. You, too, can do things you love to do, be with people you love to be with, and spend time in places that you love to be in. Do not be the one to grow old saying, "If only. . ." You have just one chance at this life, so make it a thrilling one! And don't forget that to succeed, you must start somewhere as *"even a journey of a thousand leagues starts with the first step."*[18] Take that first step today and enjoy your ongoing journey to success.

References

*" The key to happiness
is having dreams.
The key to success is making
your dreams come true. "*

~ James Allen,
poet and author
(1864-1912)

ENDNOTES

1. J. Martin Kohe, *Your Greatest Power* (Cleveland, Ohio: The Ralston Publishing Company, 1953), 9.

2. Napoleon Hill, *Think and Grow Rich* (Meriden, Connecticut: Ralston Publishing, 1938), 95.

3. Hill, 95.

4. The origins of the work on the four levels of competency are unclear. However, Gordon Training International has been instrumental in promotion of this work.

5. In economics, the J-curve principle has been used to describe the correlation between factors that result in an initial downward movement, followed by a dramatic upward progression. In his book *The J Curve Principle*, Ian Bremmer uses this principle to describe the fall and rise of nations as they move towards democracy. The J-curve principle has also been used to map the worsening and, then, the improving of a country's trade deficit after its currency was devalued. Initially, the country's citizens (let's say they come from Country A) still buy almost the same amount of foreign goods they once did, but now they must spend more to do so. This higher price paid to the foreign country (we'll call it Country B) to buy almost the exact same number of goods as before, exceeds the decrease in the volume of goods bought from Country B. Eventually, citizens of Country A will seek substitutes for the more expensive foreign products. At the same time, the "foreigners" who've been exporting to Country A, will now buy more from Country A. Country A, whose currency was devalued, now offers its products at a lower price than it once did. These two scenarios merge resulting, first, in the trade balance evening out and, then, in the favouring of Country A, the nation that had been worse off than Country B. The J-curve describes the path of the trade balance for the country with the devalued currency— negative, and then positive.

6. William Shakespeare, *The Tragedy of Hamlet, Prince of Denmark*, (Fairfield, Iowa: 1st World Library, 2005), Act III, Scene IV, line 176.

7. William James, "The Gospel of Relaxation," *Scribner's Magazine*, XXV (1899), 500.

8. Brian Tracy, *Thinking Big* (New York, New York: Simon and Schuster Audio Division, 1997).

9. Tracy

10. Marianne Williamson, A *Return to Love* (New York, New York: HarperCollins Publishers Inc., 1992), 165.

11. Maya Jaggi, "The Power of One," *GuardianUnlimited*, 13 February 1999, http://www.guardian.co.uk/weekend/story/ 0,,312252,00.html#article_continue

12. Hugh Esten, ed., "Oprah Winfrey Interview," *Academy of Achievement*, 21 February 1991 & 22 October 2006, http://www.achievement.org/autodoc/page/win0int-1 (22 October 2006).

13. Denis Waitley, *The Psychology of Winning* (New York, New York: Berkley Books, 1984), 146.

14. Dyson. "The Dyson Story," Dyson Web site and homepage. http://www.dyson.co.uk/jd/default.asp?sinavtype=menu (6 November 2006).

15. Dyson. "News Archive," *Dyson Web site*, http://www.dyson.co.uk/news/article.asp?mode=Back&id=147 (25 May 2006).

16. Luisa Kroll and Allison Fass, "The World's Billionaires, #746 James Dyson," *Forbes.com*, http://www.forbes.com/lists/2006/10/6BFC.html (6 February 2006).

17. Jim Rohn, Treasury of Quotes (Deerfield Beach, Florida: Health Communications Inc., 1996), 97.

18. Chinese proverb often attributed to Lao-Tzu

BIBLIOGRAPHY

Canfield, Jack. *The Success Principles: How to Get from Where You Are to Where You Want to Be*. New York, New York: HarperCollins Publishers Inc., 2005.

You Can

If You Believe You Can, You Can
If you think you are beaten—you are.
If you think you dare not—you don't.
If you want to win but think you can't,
It is almost a cinch you won't.

If you think you'll lose—you've lost.
For out in the world we find
That success begins with a fellow's will;
It's all in the state of mind.

Life's battles don't always go
To the stronger or faster man;
But sooner or later the man who wins
Is the one who thinks he can.

~ Unknown